LITTLE BEAST

Sara Quinn Rivara

Riot in Your Throat
publishing fierce, feminist poetry

Copyright © Sara Quinn Rivara 2023

No part of this book may be used or performed without written consent from the author, if living, except for critical articles or reviews.

Rivara, Sara Quinn.
1st edition.
ISBN: 978-1-7361386-7-0

Cover Art: Kier in Sight (unsplash.com)
Cover Design: Kirsten Birst
Book Design: Shanna Compton
Author Photo: Sara Quinn Rivara

Riot in Your Throat
Arlington, VA
www.riotinyourthroat.com

*To Jonah, always
and to Rob and Dashiell*

CONTENTS

9 Wolf
10 Leda After the Swan
13 Housewitch
15 Witch-Wife
16 Instead
18 Marvel
19 Winter Aubade
20 from *The Women's Book of Revelations*
21 Mulier Amicta Sole
22 How to Become a Miracle-Working Saint
23 Sign, Virtue, Wonder
24 Eve in the Wilderness
25 Back When I Lived in Eden
26 Instructions for Surviving the End of the World
29 Medusa
30 Bevy
31 Tornado Weather
32 Lent
33 Hermione Remembers Helen
34 My Mother the Bear
37 Elegy for the Old Gods
38 Annunciation
40 At the Far Edge of Paradise
42 Husk
43 Antihistory
44 Domestic Beast
45 Awe
46 When I Say Love I Mean El Greco's *The Assumption of the Virgin*
48 Love Song, Cannon Beach
50 Love Poem, SE Portland

51 Talisman
54 Apocrypha
55 Augury
59 Malus Domestica
63 Ha-Ha
65 Still Life
66 Bird Poem
68 Miracle
69 Little Beast

72 Acknowledgments & Thanks
74 About the Author
75 About the Press

WOLF

He had a gun. Rather, he had his pants undone. Beach-maple forest all the way down the dunes. Hoary puccoon grew along the dune trail that spiraled toward the lake. We met in a garden where tea roses bloomed. Boxwood around the lawn, three apple trees. Cheap champagne. He offered me a drink, a plate of fruit. Who was I to refuse? I was hungry. All the girls were. Girls like me, none of us beauties. And the night wore on and lights twinkled in the trees. He said he'd walk me home, touched my arm, my hair. Let his hand slip. My feet tripped. He pressed my belly into the dirt. My new dress, a jagged tear. Worms and morels in my mouth. Then he was done and I was light as air. There are ways a woman can disappear and stay right here. A nightjar called above the sycamore tree. Do you think it was my fault? A girl like me tastes like salt.

LEDA AFTER THE SWAN

I bought a pregnancy test at the party store near the river where a man was found floating face down, and before the ambulance arrived I touched his skin, cold and pink as the tile of the Elks Lodge bathroom where afterwards I stopped to pee. The bar was full. There were bushtits in the cedar that rasped its branches against the bathroom window, cigarette smoke fuzzed the walls like moss. When I walked past the men at the bar, one of them slipped his hand up my skirt and called me sweetie, another whistled at me like a bird. My throat swelled shut. A bushtit makes a nest out of moss, lichen, strands of human hair, then abandons it after the eggs are hatched. A pregnancy test takes three minutes. I reapplied my mascara, bit my lips until they bled. The sky pinked, drained into the river. A small pink cross appeared, faint and tremulous, on the plastic test. The door squeaked on its hinge as it swung shut. At the bar, a man put his hand on my leg. I let him. I know you have stories about women like me.

CONFESSION

What did I know of loss
though I had stocked
my life with it:
a husband who hated me,
nights in the fishing cabin
beneath a shallow sky,
a poker game and porn
on the living room television
while I slept off a fever,
empty beer bottles
on dirty tables.
Sex meant leaving
a body I hated
for its insistence on existing.
A curdle of blood
on the crotch
of my new lace panties
my husband bought
at Frederick's of Hollywood,
so I would transform
into something more fuckable.
Still, how I hated that word
panties, how a man
can claim anything:
a tree for felling,
a woman's small shoulders
beneath his hands, the horizon
he could tie into a noose
or unfurl into a road.
How can you lose

what you never believed
you deserved? The self
is an abandoned orchard,
windfall apples fermenting
in the late August sun.
I did not understand
until long after
that I too
was a song
worth
singing.

HOUSEWITCH

I don't care if dinner
is cooked just right if

there's enough beer to last
the night if this poem

will make him mad.
I tied a red string around my wrist

so I wouldn't forget
the first house

every window nailed shut
and I won't stick around

when this spell shrivels his dick
like a kidney bean

and the bumper rusts off his truck
and his face begins to look

like a bloated tick. I won't bother
with sorry, won't flatten my tits

wear turtlenecks so no other man
will look at me. I've forgotten

the angle my neck should bend
in supplication.

I am not allowed
to say his name but I have cursed it.

I haven't showered in weeks.
I have painted my lips candy apple red.

The only name I answer to
is wildness. The garden dirt

left half-moons beneath
my fingernails and like

the rats I've grown
to love I've burrowed

beneath the house and gnawed
the wires until
they spark—

WITCH-WIFE

God is the one unhinged, coddling his jar of unborn children. He's picking his teeth with a pin. He's done with the swan, the bull. For me he'll be himself, the monster. I've kohled my eyes, hiked my tits to my chin. Or

maybe I'm making this up and I'm in the living room eating Doritos and drinking cheap gin. The lamps are off. I haven't washed my hair in weeks. The children are fine. The children haven't made a sound. What comes next is *violence* and *then*.

Let me unzip my woman's skin. My damp animal. Moss grows on my clothes. Bees hive in my mailbox. No one pays the bills; the water's shut off. The dishes cracked. I burned the roast. No one is coming. I'm all alone.

                    This is a woman's story. You know how it ends.

Let me slip into something more comfortable. A deer carcass split down the middle. One high-heeled shoe. Let me put on my princess dress, my hot-dog costume.

I'm all teeth. I have unpetaled. Some things are meant to stay broken. God says I should keep my mouth shut but the blackflies pried it open.

INSTEAD

The field is full of starlings, the air
hazy with wings. The baby asleep

in the bassinet. The baby has my ears,
my philtrum; bow-lipped

he looks nothing like god.
For years I believed in heaven.

That what happened did not happen:
there was no fist against my throat, no violence,

no burns. No hurt. That it was my fault.
I learned to repeat: *I am unfuckable,*

I am unlovable, I am lucky
he loves me at all, for what is worse

than a woman alone? God bossed me
from the couch. I learned to want

nothing but apples. What is desire
but a road, a pile of stones?

The world was terrible. A woman's
body is a vessel, a sieve. If I could

do it again when the angel arrived
to tell me my fate I would stuff

his pretty mouth with cockleburs.
I would shove him out the door.

I would point to the field where
birds were eating the seed-corn,

tell him *those are not birds,*
but flames.

MARVEL

This is a story about motherhood, not miracles.
I cannot swim but taught swimming lessons

for three summers in high school. My first husband
once swung a hatchet above my head while the woods sang

with spring peepers. When my son's face disappeared
beneath the water at the YMCA pool then came up

panicked, I pulled him out and we never went back.
When his father peeled out of the K-Mart parking lot

and all I could see was gravel flying, my son's red
and terrified face in the passenger window, there was nothing

I could do but watch. In my dreams I swim for miles. A selkie
can return to herself if she finds her skin in a locked drawer.

I call my boy Bird though neither of us can fly.

WINTER AUBADE

Sour milk, an unmade bed. A woman asleep in a falling-down house in Paw Paw, Michigan. Yard blurred with snow. The world is burning, even so. The barn, the blackberry thicket, the house where I learned *rape*. Learned no. Everything becomes normal after a while. The child's bed, broken teacup, a length of rope. I woke up and the pond had frozen over. The sheets were dirty. I turned on all the lights. I lit the stove. Animals starting coming out of the woods: rabbit, doe, a murder of crows. The kettle sang, thin and flat. A child wept in the back room. Television tuned to static. The house grew warm, then hot. Snow sloughed off the roof. If you give a woman a match, she'll light it. The smallest things are the first to burn.

FROM *THE WOMEN'S BOOK OF REVELATIONS*

A boy chased a pickup down a gravel drive. The driver had no eyes, a
thin line where a mouth should be. I chased the boy. He tossed a Frisbee
and a small dog bit his heel. *Be careful, be careful!* I yelled. The wind

carried my voice. The boy couldn't hear. The man kept driving. What was I
but a woman in a field, pearly everlasting growing between the rows?
The sun was going down. Dusk gathered like soot around my ankles.

Will the boy be safe when night comes, so young and soft at the edge? The man
will be back wearing his necklace of teeth, mouth a black hole. Sour flowers
in his greasy palms. The sun kept its descent. We must be fierce. The man

will be back. The smell of manure a sweet field-cloud. A straight wind blew.
The truck disappeared over the hill. Something angry will be back. The boy cried.
The dog stood still. I gathered them in my arms and began to sing, low and wild.

MULIER AMICTA SOLE

A dog came out of the woods. Her side bled. A storm was coming.
I stood on the porch of the house, my son pressed his body into mine.
Wind scuttled leaves across the yard. Inside the house, some-

thing crashed. A sound like a beer can cracked. The dog howled.
My son whimpered, licked his lips. Behind us, the doorknob rattled. The air
smelled like cedar and salt and the ocean turned itself over at the bottom

of the cliff. Before I could speak his father crashed through the door.
My son howled like a wolf. The dog nuzzled my hand and my son grew fur
on his neck. The father tried to pull us back inside. He cried and cried.

The sky blacked. He would not let go of my child. The dog whimpered
then bit my hand. The father flashed his yellow teeth. I wanted to
be undone. *What now?* I asked the dog. The woods yawned. My son

dug his fingernails into my arm. The dog howled *run*—

HOW TO BECOME A MIRACLE-WORKING SAINT

Just small wonders at first: unstale the bread, find the lost keys,
match the socks, the children's rooms clean. The wedding dress

embroidered with seashells and weighted with stones. Next, try
something with feathers: a vase into a bird, a fist stuffed with eggs.

Electricity takes work: a spark from a wool sock, a table lamp, heat
lightning. Eventually the entire storm, hailstones, twister. Then blood

in the baby's milk. The truck stuck in the gravel drive and the engine
overheating, the gears grinding. Or the truck off a cliff. Or the truck

heading away, the baby safe in your arms. Try the sound of the ocean,
even here. Salt air. An inlet crowded with herons. Two crows at the edge

of the surf. You were the girl left for dead, your dress torn to shreds: out
of the dark knit the slit in your throat, balm the bruise on your thigh. Walk

into the clearing; there are blackberries. Scree, then sand. Let
the ocean rise to meet you. Clench your life between your teeth.

SIGN, VIRTUE, WONDER

As a sign there shall be a woman's hand slashed
with a steak knife, wedding dress dropped in a heap
in a beat-up blue trailer. Robin's egg blue.
Storm-sky blue. The yard hums with bees: wild carrot,
bergamot, strangleweed. The silks yellowed
at the edge as dead leaves. As a virtue
the woman bleeds and bleeds from her *wherever*.
She opens the window, kicks out the screen,
leaves. What is family but another kind
of loneliness? What we come from, Eden,
dirt, the abyss. A wonder: child at the bathroom
sink, bloody spittle. He sings his mother's name.
Miracles take work. I pulled us up and out—
a kind of hope that borders on the obscene.

EVE IN THE WILDERNESS

I could have been good. Could have kept my hair long, kept my head down, apologized more. Thrown myself in the Soo Locks, left my baby alone with a man who mowed rabbits' nests into shreds in the long grass. Stayed where the Lake lapped the beach like a woman's tongue, stayed married the first time, could have let myself die and be the girl everyone wanted me to be. I rubbed oil on the baby's head, let him run through the dunes till marram grass scraped his knees, collected his milk teeth. The sky was heavy and men shot at deer, at whatever moved in the woods. We could hear the wet thump of a body hitting the dirt. My boy clung to me, a cocklebur. A terror. Good girls know they are husk, garlic scape in wet woods, rabbit limp in the dog's hot mouth. Once I believed in God. But I am not good. I know how to bird-bone my body and holy-dove myself over the walls, whet my tongue, spit, fight. I didn't always know. My god of loam and salt, god of soft tits, heavy-bellied and tender, sits by the ocean where I have taken my child to teach him a different way to be. I could have let God kill me. Maybe He did. But I opened my mouth and the Holy Spirit flew out.

BACK WHEN I LIVED IN EDEN

There used to be three apple trees, a milk snake in henbit. Mildew bloomed. One morning I let the dogs into the backyard and they disappeared into the woods. Turkey buzzards rode thermals above the paper mill. I folded myself up the size of a girl. The mill fell in on itself. Wind tore through the orchard. Then, rain on the maples. The baby milk-drunk. Turns out, I was a thing I could have loved. Raccoon in the trash heap. The snake around my neck whispers *eat*. Don't you wish these things ended with something other than marriage or murder? The dogs have been dead for years. I walked out of that life. The girl I was had a Bowie knife in her heart. Now I hold it between my teeth. May every woman be a furious bird.

INSTRUCTIONS FOR SURVIVING THE END OF THE WORLD

The road to Mouth Cemetery is gravel, hardly a road. Runs past a falling-down yellow farmhouse, three air conditioners thrumming in the windows, a sign nailed to a dead oak: *Trespassers will be shot!* The road slips into beech-maple woods, becomes dirt, then disappears into long grass. Over the dune, Lake Michigan sluices the beach.

Everyone here has been dead for centuries. Mary, dead in childbirth. Candace, dead in childbirth, Esther, dead in childbirth, fifteen years old. Isabella, Lizzie, Albertine, Maudelle. *Wife-of.* All the babies unnamed.

One decaying obelisk leans into the weeds. Bees hum around the edges. Somebody's husband.

*

At the grocery store, a man in a camouflage hat offered to buy me a drink at the bar across the street, blocked my cart against a bin of apples. Golden delicious. *Come on, sweetie,* he said. His muscles twitched beneath a white t-shirt.

*

My son once found the skeleton of a fish at the beach and brought it home in an old mayonnaise jar. We put it on the shelf in the kitchen. His bedroom had a green smell. Nightmares are green, but darker. He slept only in my bed.

*

I heard the buckle of his belt jangle as the neighbor walked up the driveway. I was pulling weeds, eight months pregnant. Bindweed snaked between the tomatoes. When I looked up, his dick lay against his thigh. I could feel the baby swimming. *Keep working,* the neighbor said, *I just want to watch.* I could hear the rattle of my first husband's truck down the street. If we are caught, whose fault will it be?

*

Before I was a mother, I was sorrow. Then my mouth was full of Petoskey stones.

My father once shoved another man's head into a toilet at a honky-tonk bar for whistling at my mother. This was just another story I heard about love.

*

If we are caught or not, it is my fault.
I am just trying to look at my hands in the dirt.
(It is always my fault.)

*

My son never knew me to be married to his father. He slept with his feet wedged beneath my hip for nine years. If I got up he would cry. He asked, *did you know birds abandon their nests after their fledglings are big enough to fly*? I held his hand in mine.

The nights he wasn't with me, I slept curled around the dog who whimpered and twitched when he dreamed.

*

At twenty-five I put my fist through the bathroom mirror and my first husband told me I was crazy. At forty I sat alone in my car near midnight and considered pointing it into traffic. There were cedar waxwings that morning in the snowball bush. My boy drew me the skeleton of a raccoon. My second husband texted *please come home I love you it will be okay you are safe*. When I came home I smelled like water.

*

The doctor tells me I look good for a woman who's had a child. My throat hurts, a small fever. He runs his tongue over the smooth white pebbles of his teeth. Outside the window, the cemetery sun-blanched, humming. *Open wide*, he says. The clinic smells of Old Spice, soap. Stethoscope cold on my clavicle. He clears his throat. His white-coated voice: *You'll need to take off your shirt.*

MEDUSA

When I was young
and upset my mother

would turn my face
to the mirror and tell

me how ugly I looked
when I cried.

Don't think
I didn't learn something
from that.

BEVY

a collective noun of quails and ladies

Big-breasted girls, pale, we lived on Oreos and ginger
ale. The North Branch of the Chicago River hightailed it

toward the Big Lake. Everything disappeared, was swallowed up.
Trash, dead leaves, girls. We pissed in the shallow creek,

burned ants beneath a magnifying glass. *Burned them to death,*
we said. *Killed them to death!* Death was a kind of instead;

instead of eating we'd run, drink Diet Coke, break. I broke
my Deaf sister's fingers with our bedroom door. She couldn't speak

for weeks. I hit another sister on the head with a hairbrush, blood spattered
the floor. I was punished; she has a scar. Another sister I flung against

the armoire. One broke my rib, another cut the crotches from my panties
and we sliced our pictures from the yearbook, scratched out our eyes

with a tack. Boone's Farm and acetone soaked our clothes.
We'll burn if you get too close. The female body is a wet mess.

By seventeen, we'd learned to sugar our tongues, shape our fingers
around *yes*. We pressed our soft bodies against our narrow beds.

It would have been handy, learning to speak. But nobody told us that, then.

TORNADO WEATHER

Our fathers smoked Marlboro Lights, cradled sweaty cans of Bud while the tornado klaxons keened over flat grass, AM radio tuned to the Cubs game and the sky a marbled bruise. When a thin yellow light fell on our shoulders, the world went still. Water pooled beneath the viaduct over Deerfield Road while the Metra pounded overhead. On the horizon, the Chicago skyline trembled. The Lake foamed.

Only our grandparents went to Mass; we found Jesus wherever He showed up. Pink insulation from the neighbor's house blew into the yard, soft as cotton candy. Where were our mothers? Setting the table, or clearing up, or heading out to bingo until the wind picked up and they ushered us into the basement, they poured Manhattans, they hid the bourbon beneath the utility sink. Their lives were neat as mice. We were girls; no one noticed us until we swelled.

Jesus loves a good time like that, everyone a little on edge, the crackle of radio static. Should we kneel, cover our necks like they taught us in elementary school, prostrate and sour with longing? Jesus always comes in a storm, Sister Luann told us. Jesus always knows when you touch yourself like that, when you slap your mother back, when you steal Almond Joys from Walgreens, when you bleed. But

when we came home wearing blue eyeshadow, our fathers called us hussies. Rosaries hung from our bedroom doorknobs. But there was that boy on the church steps, worms in the window well, how He led us there and told us not to say a word, slipped His hand beneath the waist of our shorts. How He smelled of storms, of wind, of earth.

LENT

I prefer Lent to the Resurrection, the minor key while spring burns
beneath the snow. A little longing, a little *quaresimali*, it's nice to have

the house to myself for a while. But a man returns and we're supposed
to be glad. Sure! Roll back the stone, sound the horns, Dad's home from work

and time for dinner! Steak and watery potatoes. We weren't allowed
to speak at the table. Once I did the moonwalk and called my sister *dude*

and he slapped me hard on the mouth and said *no street talk
in my house!* Grandma Betty sent us new Easter dresses: pink

and lavender gauze, satin ribbons around our waists.
We piled into the station wagon for Mass. I loved a fancy dress,

loved to spin violently until I fell and the room whizzed around me.
No spinning in church. Take the Body of Christ on your tongue.

I refused to take the dress off to play kickball in the wet grass until
I fell and a green smear bloomed across the skirt. I said the priest

looked like a frog. My father laughed, *that's my girl.* Then everyone else:
S——, we told you to be good, now look what you've become.

HERMIONE REMEMBERS HELEN

When I was pregnant with you, I only gained [x] pounds, my mother
told me when I was pregnant with my son, *and I only weighed [x] pounds*

three days after you were born. She handed me a photograph of her
in a halter top: lustrous hair, rosebud lips. She eyed my belly,

the swell of my hips. After my son was born, I bought six scales
at Target, weighed myself on each of them a dozen times a day, walked

in the swelter of summer with the baby strapped to my chest, tried to whittle
my body down to bone to nothing, to what is safe, which is to disappear.

Not every woman can be a beauty, she said. My mother
always told me to treat people the way I wanted to be treated,

which meant: if you are selfless enough, maybe somebody will love
you back. Doesn't matter who. No guarantees. Was it my first

husband who threw me against the wall, or the man who pressed
me onto the grass and pinched my nipples so hard they bled, or

the man who said *I don't know if I love you or if I love my wife?*
Mama, you are small and fierce, my son said when he was three

and crawled into bed with me. It was raining so hard outside
I could not tell if I was laughing or crying.

MY MOTHER THE BEAR

*

When my father died, there was some crying, then my mother sold the house and all of his things, moved away. We never speak of it. There was no funeral, no obituary. Sometimes, she says *I'm so sad but I should just get over it.* Other times, I can't find her at all. She doesn't answer the phone. Gets the names of her grandchildren wrong. His ashes in a tin in the back of her closet.

*

Sometimes she pretends to love what he loved: beer, tomatoes in a humid Midwestern garden, pointing the hose at zucchini. A mother-of-pearl sky. Cicadas and thunderstorms. Other times, the neighbors find her near the creek, barefoot, wearing her furs. We are not the kind of family who speaks of joy.

*

My parents smoked Marlboro Lights, served us braunschweiger on Wonder Bread, drank powdered sweet tea, Pepsi, cheap American beer. We drove from Illinois to Ohio and back again, windows rolled up, car filled with smoke. When we stopped outside Columbus to pee, my sisters and I covered the windows of the station wagon with maxi-pads. My father never said a word.

*

The last time I saw my father, he was visiting my new house on the continent's edge, thirty steps up to the porch. I was afraid it would kill him. *Hope I don't kill dad!* I joked. This is the kind of person I am. His heart was already failing.

*

My father called me, his firstborn, Bear. I heard in his voice, *my dear one.* When I called, sometimes we would talk a bit and then he'd hand the phone to my mother. Sometimes, if he'd been drinking, he would cry when he said

I love you. Now when I call my mother, sometimes the phone rings and rings. When she answers, she sounds out of breath. As if she's been crying.

*

When he died, I was not there. I did not answer the phone until my sister called me four times.

Oh fuck, oh fuck, oh fuck.

*

He took my sister and me to the Fourth of July carnival. He bought us cotton candy; my sister won a bicycle. He held our hands as we walked home, over the railroad tracks, down Hazel Avenue, down the tunnel of trees on Forest Avenue to our house. Our mother was home with the youngest girls. I thought the Fourth of July was my favorite holiday.

*

Once when he was angry, he kicked in the back door. I remember looking in the refrigerator, for milk, or seedless grapes, or cottage cheese. He told me *everyone hates their job*. When I left for college, he stood at the end of the driveway and sobbed.

*

They often locked their bedroom door, my parents. We could hear them over the TV, *Wheel of Fortune* or *Jeopardy* filling the den. We're just talking, they said. *Once your father and I broke the bed*! my mother tells me when I am twenty-three.

*

Once my mother told me, after she'd lost her job, that she wished my father had some empathy. *But that's not his job*, she said. No one gets to be happy in this life.

*

My mother spends all summer in her garden: cigarette, coneflower, tomatoes. She tells me what she has planted (rudbeckia, hosta, pansy), what is taking over (pampas grass, Rose of Sharon, so many weeds). In the winter, she stands outside the back door and rings of smoke float above her head. I can hear her inhalation over the phone, the slow breath out. *No, no, I've quit smoking*, she says. I can hear the animals circling near her fence, how patiently they wait for her to scatter birdseed in the snow. For the cats, she opens a can of tuna. For the bears, she holds out her wrists.

ELEGY FOR THE OLD GODS

The house smells of Old Spice, myrrh. The curtains drawn,
smoke curling up the chimney in a long, flaccid loop. This is
how it is when the world ends; no horsemen, no

seven-horned lamb. No one raptures the gods. Just a long,
slow evening at the edge of the neighborhood where the lights
of the strip mall filter through the trees. Look at them

long enough and they might be stars. The kitchen is filthy,
no one has vacuumed in weeks. The gods wander the living
room in their underwear, complaining about the weather.

Just because once they pinned me to the four-poster bed (one
to watch and one to pray and one to bear my soul away) doesn't mean
I am holy. They don't like the woman I've become.

I've had enough. Outside it has begun to snow.
In the city someone is ministering to the poor, someone
is being gassed by the police. We must shoulder our own burdens,

                                            the soft human weight of them.

ANNUNCIATION

I am no dish to be passed or filled, I am no
princess. I am apple, spindle, thorn, blood

on the bathroom floor, piss on the pregnancy test, pink
yesyesyes. Once upon a time a girl climbed down

from a high tower using only her hair. We make our own
ropes. The prince came upon me like a swan, blood shadow,

he covered me with his thousand wings. In his story I
waited and bowed my head, or there was a poison apple, glass

coffin, vines up the stony tower, a happilyeverafter
once I accepted my fate. My story begins with fangs.

Owls roost in the hickory. So much sugar in my milk.
Once, I grew a woman in my animal skin. She was holy

as skim milk, as sin. And then?
                                    Then the light crept in.

CLOUD/BREATH

I'm the low-slung fog over the shorn cornfield
where men in orange vests wait for a doe to wander into range
of their Remingtons. I'm the moon smeared low and bright

while hunters strew apples in the dirt. I shimmy onto the field
in my sexy deer costume, then light the dry earth on fire,
my mouth full of gasoline. A life

in Paradise wasn't for me: all day, the television blares
and God tromps around in his boxers with a warm beer.
Animals wander, empty-headed and lonely.

I paint my eyelids Lake Superior blue, float in a cloud of Aqua Net,
make my church a wasps' nest high in the eaves. Let me gather the beasts
and set them free. Let me hang my godhead

in the cedar and slip naked into the cold river. Let me be
the kind of gods who care enough
                                              to look back on what I've abandoned.

AT THE FAR EDGE OF PARADISE

Dear X—

Today my son said, kindly, *it's nice that you're past the age of caring how you look.* When I jerked my head up he said *no, that's not what I mean.* But it is what I mean: I am tired of writing about myself. I want

to push every poem toward something important, something that says I lived and some of it mattered, though most of living is just toilet paper and laundry, driving the same stretch of highway to the same soul-killing

job. Anyway, I'm just a minor poet in Somewhere, America where it is sleeting sideways and we're out of milk. Adam named the animals and Eve swallowed their names like pomegranate seeds before she slipped into the underworld

for a few months to get away from family life. I know—different stories but after long enough all stories with women are the same. Pink mold in the shower. Everyone wants something different for dinner and no one

thinks you're fuckable anymore. I mean me. But you're also 43, though in Somewhere Else, America, but it might be the same. Perhaps your mailbox is also full of spider eggs and in the shed a hive of bees have formed

their winter cluster around the queen, shivering and dancing to keep what's important alive. I know not everything survives. I remember waking in Venice after the midnight train from Lyon, how we thought we'd always

be friends. Well, I did. Years happened and then we didn't speak. Once, drunk, we lay on the floor of our walk-up apartment, and imagined names for our imaginary children we would have with imaginary

men. Then it was just me, my shitty first marriage, this miracle kid
and you had vacations to Puerto Rico. I imagine your immaculate
kitchen, your books alphabetized on a dustless shelf. Now, every poem

is an attempt to keep the woman I am from becoming a turnip,
a radish, a day-old ham. I am becoming someone no one can see.
It's still sleeting and the power has gone out. I apologize.

I hope it's okay I'm writing to you here in the empty garden,
everything slick with ice. Where I can see my breath, where it smells
of nothing but cold. The groaning you hear is up in the cedar

where something is singing. Something old and tired and ready to fall.

HUSK

When did my body become a seedpod, burst open and brittle? I am cavernous
with hunger. At first, I loved scotch broom blooming near the highway in June,

how yellow, how bright. The biologist next door chided *it's a blight,
chokes out anything native.* I don't tell him I love how the seedpod explodes,

launches seed further and further up the embankment, how early summer blazes
xanthic along the ordinary highway. Yet. God, I've been so sad.

Weed-fields sour in fire season. Once my lover groaned at a middle-aged poet
who read poems about the aging body. *More menopause poems, haven't we had*

enough? His eyes rolled. And because I believed I would always be opalescent
(don't we all?) I smiled and agreed, put my hand in his lap.

At some point, a woman must forget blooming, how bright the body
how violent. By late summer, only furred and withered pods hang

on the stem, seeds covering the field like stars. O, what was it I taught
my son about the stars? Once we can see their fires, they are already gone.

ANTIHISTORY

If my body is a stranger, let it make its home in the deep woods where a clear stream runs beneath cedar, fir. If it must live in a small house with the windows locked, let it know where the knives are kept and how to use them. Let it fight back. If I am a small thing, let me be fierce. If this snake is my body, let it be lethal, let me make my burrow in the weedy hillside where sedge withers and no birds sing. If I am the monster let me devour. Leave your children in the woods and I will find them and we will be wild together. Moss hangs its crumpled gown on the cedar. The sky hangs its blades between my thighs. If this skirt is too short, let me roll it shorter. If I am asking for it then I will shout. Puffball mushrooms, buzzards. The ground is wet and everywhere weeds—vetch, loosestrife, bindflower. If my body is a vessel, it overflows. Let me be the angel who speaks blackberry, sword fern, calamity. I'll flag down the next shining car and head toward the city. I'll make us all beasts.

DOMESTIC BEAST

For a time I learned to want nothing, which
is how to be a woman. Then I prepared
the small monsters of my mind.

(In my dream, my son and I are safe in the orchard,
a black snake draped over our shoulders.
We are sweet with apples)

(In my dream, a blue salamander follows me
through a flooded subway, hides in the cuff
of my jeans)

(In my dream, I have murdered a girl by cutting
her throat and I am afraid you will find
her body in the woods beneath oak leaves)

I have the head of a wolf, a woman's body.
The head of a goat and rough fingers.
Sometimes, a dappled fawn,

a doe dead in the empty woods. Sometimes
the hunter's orange cap, warm truck.
Sometimes the gun.

A woman is made of sheet cake, spun sugar, dirt.
In this dream the chickens have pinned the rat
in the corner of the coop. Soon there will be nothing but bones.

AWE

My first husband said I am a frigid whore, warned
my second husband I smell of fish. What's actually in

a name? *I* is a bruise; *she* a flower; *he* a welter. One spring
I ate only carrots and my palms turned orange. Sometimes

I run until I puke. I want bone edge instead of flesh.
God says *I love you for your smallness.* The body says *of dust*

am I made. Beneath my ribs, open fields, lilies, mackerel sky.
The body remembers even if we forget. I do not know how

to be. Deer walk into the field and are shot. Hunters rejoice.
Sunset blazes orange. Hunters drive their pickups over dusk roads.

I am the dusk road, the doe. Once, when I arrived to pick up
my son from his father's apartment, only tiny footprints

were left in the snow. My breath froze. I closed my mouth
around a stone. Eventually, my son returned, bloody-lipped.

Today, the cashier at the grocery says I seem too old for a son
who's thirteen. Somehow we made it here. I run and run

and still time outdoes me. Orion wheels in the southern sky.
By *awe* the Greeks meant wonder, but they also meant grief.

WHEN I SAY LOVE I MEAN EL GRECO'S *THE ASSUMPTION OF THE VIRGIN*

where she rises from a crowd
of men into the sky, how she throws open

her arms and floats into a cloud of gold.
She's the only woman in the room.

And isn't that
what I'm supposed to want? To be the only woman

worth lifting into the clouds, bride
on her wedding day, mayflies buzzing

around all our heads.
Mayflies have no mouths.

Chicago is chiaroscuro
this time of year when light is eaten

by the lake and salt stains
our legs. But maybe

the angels are women,
who can tell, beauty is cold.

Them: swallow-winged and radiant,
round and rosy cheeked, maybe

this is where all the women go,
raptured up to heaven

with our men and their guns
our lipstick and our big tits.

Up here with the angels and the dead
it smells like Pine Sol and bleach. My first marriage

bares its tiny cubic zirconium
teeth. Sundogs spiral over the Lake.

When I say *love* it means
I'm supposed to carry everything

and I'm afraid I'll kill it.

LOVE SONG, CANNON BEACH

My son tells me to stick my finger
in an open anemone though it might sting.

On Haystack Rock, tufted puffins return
each year to lay eggs and raise their young.
Cells divide but not forever.

Mom, do you remember before me? The tide
is coming in. He's wet to the knees.
I think I have always been here.

My new husband and his son make sandcastles
while we watch starfish slip beneath the waves.

The sandcastle goes under. There is no before,
no after. The boys trace stars into the sand,

run into a crowd of gulls. *How do jellyfish live
without brains?* they ask. We eat ice-cream
for dinner, walk barefoot back to the hotel.

The boys talk until midnight. Our bodies taste
like salt. Tree frogs sing through the open window.

My husband hums and puts the boys to bed.
To call a thing by name is a kind of spell:

Mom, S—, love. Even so, the past wolf-whistles
bitch, unlovable. Fog rolls in, smears the panes.
Today the ocean is calm. Tomorrow,

the weather will shift. Big rollers, north wind.
One rogue wave could swallow us.

LOVE POEM, SE PORTLAND

My husband tells me he saw a coyote race down 26th Street
while he waited for his son outside the middle school. A cougar

killed a woman on Mt. Hood. Everyone is hungry these days.
Fire-scorched Gorge means when the rains come, everything

could slide: houses, animals forced into the valley. I once
had a husband who called me Dog, who told me he'd chop

me into pieces if I left. How do I tell *this* husband I saw a doe
field-dressed and strung from a gambrel, a man peel her skin

from her joints in one swift tear? I told that man I loved him
because I was afraid. How do I tell this man and our sons

who are watching a cowboy astronaut movie and eating pizza,
are barefoot and safe in our warm bungalow, that wasps nest

in the walls, bears who haven't eaten for months circle the house,
that I too am a wild thing, a lake squall, wood rot? I've bared my teeth.

S—, this husband tells me, *that coyote was running from something.*

TALISMAN

If I were gone, how would your life change? I ask a few days after our sixth anniversary. Each night you sleep with your hand on my hip, you say *I love you* as easily as a creek eases its way over basalt. I soften, sometimes, when I am with you. The waitress brings us our drinks; the floor is sticky, the window fogged with our breath.

What I am afraid of is you will say *it won't*. Instead, you put your hand over mine.

✶

When we were first married, we took our boys to the woods. They were eight and had their struggles. You taught them each to throw a leaf off a bridge and let them race with the current, a slow meander. Sometimes the leaves would get stuck in an eddy, sometimes they would float away toward the sea. The boys' faces pink with cold.

When I first came to visit you, we woke late in the morning. Two crows perched on the neighbor's roof and looked at us through the open window. One for sorrow, two for joy.

✶

Often, I ask you if you still love me. You are constant, unable to lie. I do not always understand this, how you can be rooted so true to yourself. *Please come back, I miss you* you tell me one night in our first summer, when I have disappeared into myself. I had sent my son 1,800 miles away with his father for two months, and my heart was shattered. I replay this, a loop. *Come back, I love you.* There is such gentleness. When my son comes home, you hug both our boys with ease.

By the time of our seventh anniversary, we have been quarantined for six months. I have stopped wearing makeup, your hair froths about your head in a silver cloud. The boys are almost as tall as you, can rest their chins on the top of my head.

✶

Early in the pandemic, the power went out and we sat at the dining room table and played board games with the boys. Later, you showed them how to string a guitar. Later, I gathered the chickens off the fence and shut them in the coop. The air was warm even after the sun went down. We sat on the porch drinking whiskey.

Later, you made us dinner and we told each of our sons *I love you* and sent them upstairs for bed.

✶

When I was twenty-eight, a man held me down by my throat and told me only he could love me. Our baby screamed in his bassinet by the bed.

✶

When we are in bed, you curl around me, and the cats curl at our feet.

✶

I understand only how to practice for catastrophe.
It is easier to imagine what can go wrong than what can bloom. What I have learned is: *don't get your hopes up*. What you have learned is: *hope is necessary*.

✶

Once, I lay on the polished wood floor of my apartment afraid anything I loved would be taken away from me. I did not understand the nature of abundance.

✶

Once, when we first started dating, I sprawled naked across the couch, looked right at the camera. When you woke, 1,800 miles away and four hours later, there I was, naked on your screen.

✶

Once, we married each other beneath a weeping linden tree.
Once I believed I would never be safe.

✶

Once, my grandmother broke open a sand dollar she'd brought back from Florida to show me how God was in all things: *look,* she said, *see how inside there are doves, the holy spirit,* and shook into my hand five bone birds. In me, the holy spirit burned a blue flame.

APOCRYPHA

After my father died I dreamed my husband
left me. He loaded cats, chickens, clothes

into an old black truck. It was snowing. He pressed
two warm eggs into my hands and drove away.

At breakfast, our sons and I discussed the universe:
always expanding or shrinking. At any rate infinite

and glittering. I am late to everything except love.
We spent the afternoon feeding ducks at the city

pond. Buffleheads, wigeons, mallards, wood ducks
followed our trail of seed corn. The boys whooped,

threw handfuls in a jubilant arc above our heads.
My father is still dead and so is the black dog

I rescued back in Michigan, so is the chicken
the dog murdered days before the dog's heart

burst. His gums were white and my husband
carried him down the steps like a bride.

AUGURY

To begin is a bird. Knife-wound sky. A bruise. The wet expanse of a spring morning—daffodil, bloodroot. You are folding laundry; hummingbirds buzz the viburnum. I don't know how to ask you to help me to not be afraid.

✶

There is a straight line in my mind between occurrence and calamity. If there is a gun in the first act, by the third someone will be dead. I know how stories work: no one locks it away, forgets it in a drawer, removes it from the house forever. Why mention it if you don't mean it? What I mean is: I must prepare myself for the worst. Three chickadees at the feeder, scrub jay in the cedar.

✶

Your shoes left wet smears on the sidewalk: five minutes' walk to the hospital, the cheery nurses, the radiation machine. You text me a picture: someone stuck an Oompa-Loompa sticker to the peaceful lake above the table. When I imagine it, though, what I see is only water.

✶

For dinner we eat toast and new eggs, a glass of whiskey. The scent of cherry blossoms drifts through the screen. Our life hangs in-between, mist strung on cedar. At night I origami myself small as a bird. Your hands caress my shoulders. You kiss my neck.

✶

On the way to work, I see cormorants crouched on a dead tree in the river, brown with spring runoff. All the streams are fast and cold and I read miracles everywhere: heron in the pond, the tarot which says *fecundity, blessing, sword*. Fear salts my tongue. *Let me see a bird if…* I ask. I don't know if it is prayer, or riddle, or spell. Three hawks on highway lamp-posts. Seventeen crows in the deodar cedar.

*

The first thing I noticed when I moved to Portland was a river of crows streaming across the evening sky, how slowly they hopped out of the road despite my approaching car. Woodsmoke smelled different than the Midwest where I had been lonely. Hellebore and witch hazel blooming. In the afternoon after the radiation room, you pick up our boys from school. I think: *how strange it is to feel safe.*

*

To begin is the bloodrose of radiation, the cold quiet of the cancer-center lobby. The litany of doctors, surgeons, radiologists. I fill a notebook. So many men nodding. At night, you sleep easily and smell of wet earth, summer air.

*

What I was prepared for was my own breakage; a return of cells blooming on my cervix, everything I'd done in twenty years taken away from me. I did not expect you to be on the table. *Maybe you should have,* my worst mind tells me. *You can't expect joy.*

*

Love burns a small circle between my breasts.

*

Time churns into cream. Back at the hospital, *oncology, brachytherapy, prostate, metastasis* slide over our tongues like peeled eggs. Then you are wheeled off, and I wait for your number to appear on the little screen: prep, in surgery, in recovery. Somewhere, radiation blooms inside of you, little seeds, rosettes of light.

*

Starlings and house sparrows argue in the bushes by the sliding doors of the cancer ward. I wait for hours while the doctors put a hundred radioactive seeds inside your body. When I asked them if you will glow in the dark, nobody laughs but you.

In the parking garage, a thrush sings. When you wake up, you flirt with the nurses. You lean on my arm, hum a little when we drive home, then whimper as I help you up the stairs and into the dark bedroom. So many song sparrows in the trees.

Any place seems like home after a while, so why not hope? Maybe there is no gun. Maybe it is locked away. Maybe no one will take it out and use it today.

To begin is a bird. Cormorant, scrub jay, vireo. Two great blue herons perched above Beaver Creek I want to believe mean *it's okay*. Mean *relax into this good life*. But. I want to tell you a prayer: how hope works like a scythe, a flower unfurling into bloom, a tree swallow returning each spring, wings curved as knives—

WAKING MY SON FOR SCHOOL

He leaves the curtains pulled shut, the window open
even in winter. Light filters thin as old leaves
across the bed. His bedroom smells of rain. The old dog curls
around him, and one of the cats sleeps by his head.

I know a white man is a ticking time bomb. Can be. Might.
His drawings of a cassowary skull and a fish skeleton crumpled
on the floor. Dirty socks, a pile of shoes. Once, we drove
seven hours north to Mackinac Island, stood with our feet

in the Straights and filled our pockets with limestone
pebbles to skip across the water. Water a mirror. Water
a stone. Once he swam inside of me, lake perch, minnow—
but all boys leave their mothers. All boys are told they must

become men. Once we walked beneath the carnival lights
at the county fair and listened to the screams of other people's
children on the Tilt-a-Whirl. It is getting late; there is only an hour
before school. In the half-light, his face still looks like mine.

I know the trick is to stay in my body when all I feel
is the rising panic in my chest the way the carnival Zipper
flings itself over the Bi-Mart parking lot, lights smeared
across the wet asphalt, the way a boy becomes a man, the way

the heart is a hard apple, so sweet it hurts.

MALUS DOMESTICA

I was afraid all the time. In the end, I think motherhood makes you obscene.
—Marguerite Duras

✶

A man once told me he was going to write a novel about a trucker who was lost in the median scrub somewhere up north. *It's ten yards across, how could he not find his way out?* I asked but men are right about every idea. *I could fight a bear if I needed to*, he said over his shoulder while we hiked through November woods.

A man said, *you can't tell anyone you have an STD, because they will know I gave it to you.*

A man said after my exam, *I felt your cervix and you're definitely not pregnant, I've been doing this a long while, you're probably just stressed.* Three days later, a pink cross on the test.

A man called my midwife, told her I was crazy, asked if there were pills. *You're my wife, you are supposed to have sex with me, there is something wrong with you, are you frigid, are you crazy.* I learned the art of being small, smaller.

A man said, over dinner, *It would be better if you didn't write about having cervical cancer. If you didn't write that your ex gave you an STD. What if my grandmother reads it? What would she think of me?*

A man got up early to work on his muscles. He cooked me one square of tempeh, a half-cup of frozen peas. *No carbs after noon*, he said. *You'll balloon.* My ribs pressed at my skin.

A man said *if you didn't leave me then you'd have your son all the time, what kind of a mother are you, a bad one.* The baby came home with bruises, rug burns across his back.

A man is a multitude: fox, wolf, bear; cook, lawyer, cop, professor. *I like to watch a woman while she cleans.*

You would be easier to love if you weren't already a mother a man told me in bed. He stroked my soft belly. *You can tell you had kids.*

A man said *you are too much.*

✶

When the midwife told me I was pregnant with a boy, I was terrified it meant I would lose him too. I meant, lose me. The only way to be a man was to be terror.

The first few years, I was terrified that I would leave the baby in the car; that I would wake and he would not be breathing beside me; that I was the woman the man said I must be.

What is a mother but a bad dream? A person who undoes the hours.

Cinderella, dressed in yella, went downtown to meet a fella. Made a mistake, kissed a snake, how many doctors did it take?

What was I? A woman with a body that belongs to everybody else. The child ate apples, climbed trees, slept in the empty bed beside me. He tucked his feet beneath my hip. When he woke crying, he let his hand settle in mine. I cleared my life of a certain kind of desire.

✶

Imagine there is an orchard just off the highway. Imagine that the bottle has rolled beneath the passenger seat and the baby's feet just reach your back, and you can reach your hand back and hold his heel in your palm.

Shorn cornfields roll past the windows, empty and dry. You are the only single mother here. Time accordions itself: you are thirty and then you are forty-five.

Sometimes the orchard is covered by a thin haze, sometimes it's thick fog. Some days the sky so blue it could knife you clean through.

There is a barn, an old dappled steer near a pile of rotting apples studded with bees. A hen with a train of chicks in the long grass between the steer's legs.

Imagine labor then milk then the baby is a toddler, a boy, a young man with a soft beard.

A boy, fifteen, angular. He throws small, hard fruit at your feet and then shimmies up a tree, then leaps down, then throws his arm over your shoulder. Imagine you both look up, and see airplane float over the hills, low and large, silent. It disappears behind the ridgeline.

Did you see it, Mom? he asks, incredulous. *Is it a ghost plane? Maybe it's a ghost plane.* For a moment, he lets his head rest on your shoulder. Imagine a tender place between your ribs.

The plane floated behind the clouds. The steer stomped in the grass.

✶

Imagine you are, if you can, a mother. It involves an undoing. Imagine you are responsible for everything.

Imagine a man once said *I love you* or *I love your body but not your mind* or *I am not sure if I love you or if I love my wife* or *the heart wants what the heart wants*. Imagine he says you are a bad mother for leaving. It is your fault, everything. Imagine you walk away, into the orchard, your son on your hip, your hands sticky, your belly soft.

Imagine you got lost in a corn maze and your boy rode on your shoulders until you found a way out. Both of you crying. You stuffed our mouths with donuts when you were free.

You're a strong little mama, he told me.

HA-HA

Sometimes when we are fucking and my husband
puts his large, gentle hands on my collarbone I think:
he could strangle me if he wanted. Sometimes

I have to sit on my hands because I am compelled
to swallow my wedding ring. That's funny, I think,
weird, as in funny, as in a hedge apple grown

wild and fruiting along the fencerow. Once
a student opened his large palm
when I told him to stop interrupting me, and there

rattled two bullets. Once a man wouldn't stop
sending me pictures of his dick, and pictures of his wife
who was dead in a car accident. *Oops,* he would text,

not meant for you. Then for whom? Once a boyfriend
told me I must have been a good wife to my first husband because
from what he could tell, I just *went along with everything*

and asked if my first marriage was some kind of performance
art. Once a boyfriend told me he could fight a bear
if he wanted to. Once a dean told me the student

who showed up at my house was *just curious* and called
him *your little friend* and suggested if I didn't like
that kind of attention I might change the way I dress.

Once my first husband said *you're beautiful except
for when you speak.* Sometimes in the blue hours
of night I can't remember if I'm a girl or a boy

and my second husband lets his hand rest on my hip
and in the poem I'm reading by a poet who is braver
than me, she describes her lover:

her stretch marks, like inlaid mother of pearl.

STILL LIFE

I spent all morning digging up the tree of heaven in the garden. *That's a stupid name for a tree*, my son tells me. Cut it down and the roots keep growing, through the foundation, through the basement walls. *I thought you said 'heathen'*

but it's still stupid. Heaven is so close to heathen, to hearth, to dirt. My children, the olden dog, my husband: hungry, what time is dinner, what's for dessert, my laundry basket is full. Dirt gathers in the kitchen corners, cabinets smeared

with fingerprints, dried tomato sauce from last night's dinner. A splatter of day-old milk from someone's cereal. Rats have tunneled into the chicken coop and raccoons sleep in the cedar. Sometimes my son folds me into his arms

and says *love you, Mom*, and his chin scrapes my scalp; sometimes I find hours to practice Bach, a few hours to pull nightshade from the flower beds, pull the summer's last tomatoes before frost. Once, I believed I would be significant,

that I would see Paris, sleep with only those who loved me, have a thin body free of sorrow. Outside the kitchen window a northern flicker lands beneath the snowball bush, asters bloom, steel gray sky. The pasta water boils.

Vanity of vanities. The house smells of garlic and rain. My body rounds itself toward the verdant earth. And my heart a thing blooming, breaking, a bird.

BIRD POEM

*

This morning I chased the chickens through the neighbor's yard and into the apartment complex wearing only my underwear and a hot pink t-shirt. I tucked them beneath my arms, calling them *dear heart, sweetling, birdie.*

*

I have called my son Bird since he was born. His name means dove in Aramaic. He was born during a difficult time.

*

My grandfather called me Tiger, another cousin he called Steamboat. In his garden, zucchinis grew as big as a man's thigh. In my father's garden, tomatoes caught the wet summer light.

*

One chicken is in perpetual molt, another refuses to lay. We cage what we love and what we want to stay. The rest we push away.

*

In two years my son will be eighteen and tonight he hugged me so hard my back cracked. Sometimes I wonder what would happen if I just collapsed.

*

The chickens have eaten the entire lawn, every green thing in the garden gone. We build a caged run. We lock them down. The new garlic spikes through the raised beds.

*

When my son was little he would ask for a rocky hug and wrap his legs around my waist. In the dark, I didn't think he could see me cry.

✳

Before my father died, he told me in high school he stole two ducklings from a neighbor, raised them in a cardboard box in the garage, with just a bare lightbulb for heat. He smelled of cigarettes and beer.

✳

In high school, my friends and I would ride hotel elevators and pretend to faint just to see the faces of the adults around us darken. One man whistled at me like a bird.

✳

A man whistled at me like a bird. Am I the bird or is the man whistling the bird?

✳

A redwing blackbird whistles only when it's warm enough to return to the marsh reeds. When it is safe.

✳

My son and I slept in the same bed for the first nine years. So we felt safe. So we. He tucked his feet beneath my knees. It was just him and me.

✳

Once a pediatrician told me it was wrong to let my toddler sleep in my bed. Let him cry it out, he said. Man up. What is that, a man? We walked out the door into a summer dusk. Sparrows dotted the lawn.

✳

Near dusk, the chickens gather near the coop. They eat corn from my open hand. Upstairs, my son plays his guitar and sings. In the darkling trees, wild birds wait to eat the fallen seed.

MIRACLE

When the starling cannon boomed, the fields around the village shook off their wings. A blue Cutlass Supreme painted with flames crashed into a cornfield and an angel staggered out, fell to her knees in the incarnate world. A man approached her with a gun and his pants unzipped. She opened the tank. She lit the match. He was a man she'd loved, or left. Ash filled the air. The angel unhinged her jaw. And the stars were bombs waiting to fall. And eight deer stepped from the trees wearing crowns, wearing the dreams of our children like robes. Light stretched between them like ropes. Thorns on their heads. The skin of the angel was gold. The neighbors locked their doors but the children slipped out. Parents ignored the warnings: the torn screen, the open window, clothes on the line full of wind where bodies had been. I felt beside me in bed but no one was there. Flames over the trees like the northern lights. Fear, undo your borders. We built the bleeding world, we hold the knife. The angel squats in the ditch and sings, her voice like smoke beneath door and sill. When our hearts break, birds fly out.

LITTLE BEAST

In the little story I tell about
myself I am sparrow, angel, the girl

pricked but not plucked, the witch and not
the body fucked. Nightshade tangled on chain

link fence. Imagine I am made of flesh.
Imagine black and oily wings. I wear

my fury like spun gold. My name translated
means *une petite bête*. Imagine I am

like you. Fear wings its way through wet woods,
animal. Imagine I am a woman,

satin dress hitched above my knees, hemmed
with honeybees, menstrual-red

and clotted with rubies. I am catastrophe,
calyx. I'm from out of town, hauling

my suitcase up your stairs. The blood washed
off the lintel in the rain. No one is safe.

ACKNOWLEDGMENTS & THANKS

Thank you to the journals where many of these poems previously appeared:
Bending Genres: "Bird Poem"
Cherry Tree Review: "Witch-Wife"
Colorado Review: "From the Women's Book of Revelations," "Apocrypha"
Crab Creek Review: "How To Become a Miracle-Working Saint"
Diode: "Husk," "At the Far Edge of Paradise"
Dunes Review: "Awe"
Gigantic Sequins: "Annunciation"
Heavy Feather Review: "Instructions for Surviving the End of the World"
Indianapolis Review: "Domestic Beast"
JMWW: "Augury"
Mom Egg Review: "Mulier Amicta Sole"
The Night Heron Barks: "Hermione Remembers Helen"
Pidgeonholes: "Talisman"
Pithead Chapel: "Antihistory"
Rogue Agent: "Leda After the Swan," "Confession"
Sugarhouse Review: "Winter Aubade"
Superstition Review: "Bevy"
Sweet: A Literary Confection: "Love Song, SE Portland," "Instead," "When I Say Love, I Mean El Greco's *Assumption of the Virgin*"
SWWIM: "Love Song, Cannon Beach"
West Branch: "Miracle" and "Little Beast"
West Trestle: "Eve in the Wilderness"
Whale Road : "Back When I Lived in Eden"

Gratitude to Lisa Gluskin Stonestreet, who read and advised on many of these poems in their infancy, to Courtney LeBlanc and Riot in Your Throat, to Megan Dugan for friendship, and always to Rob Yardumian, best first reader and love, to Jonah and Dashiell, my heart.

ABOUT THE AUTHOR

Sara Quinn Rivara is the author of *Little Beast* (Riot in Your Throat), *Animal Bride* (Tinderbox Editions), and *Lake Effect* (Aldrich Press). She lives in the Pacific Northwest with her family, cats, dog, and multiple chickens. Find her online at saraquinnrivara.com

ABOUT THE PRESS

Riot in Your Throat is an independent press that publishes fierce, feminist poetry.

Support independent authors, artists, and presses.

Visit us online:
www.riotinyourthroat.com

www.ingramcontent.com/pod-product-compliance
Lightning Source LLC
Chambersburg PA
CBHW030311100526
44590CB00012B/589